HERBAL BOUQUETS

HERBAL BOUQUETS

BY EMELIE TOLLEY AND CHRIS MEAD

CLARKSON POTTER/PUBLISHERS

NEW YORK

Published by Clarkson Potter/Publishers, New York, New York
Member of the Crown Publishing Group.

Random House, Inc. New York, Toronto, London, Sydney, Auckland
www.randomhouse.com

CLARKSON N. POTTER is a trademark and POTTER and colophon are registered trademarks of
Random House, Inc.

Printed in China

Design by Lauren Monchik

Library of Congress Cataloging-in-Publication Data
Tolley, Emelie.
    Herbal bouquets / by Emelie Tolley and Chris Mead—1st ed.
    1. Herbs—utilization.   2. Bouquets.   3. Floral decorations.
    I. Mead, Chris.   II. Title.
SB351.H5 T645 2001
745.92'5—dc21   00-038522

ISBN 0-609-60438-4

10 9 8 7 6 5 4 3 2 1

First Edition

To Charles Cashion, Richard Sutter, and Donald Wise,
whose help and support I will always appreciate.
—E.T.

To Kathy.
—C.M.

ACKNOWLEDGMENTS

Over the years many people have contributed to our knowledge and enjoyment of herbs. We're grateful to all of them, but for this current project we would particularly like to thank Sheila Chefetz, Dana Stravinsky, Patricia Trainor, Alexander Jakowec, Alex Sigmon, Albert Morris, John and Sandy Horvitz, Roderick Anderson and Blantyre, Ron Wendt, Denise Dunne, Eastlake Farms, and Jim Bibo. And as always, our thanks to our friends at Clarkson Potter, who bring our visions to reality, most especially Margot Schupf, Marysarah Quinn, and Lauren Monchik.

c o n t e n t s

a bouquet of favorites

INTRODUCTION

Bright yellow goldenrod, stately foxgloves, spectacular poppies, graceful peonies, and fragrant roses live happily side by side with mint, basil, rosemary, and chives in the herb garden. The world of herbs is far more varied than most of us realize, affording a trove of glorious blooms and foliage to use in bouquets and containers.

For thousands of years, civilizations from the Egyptians to the Chinese have used herbs and herbal flowers in celebrations and religious rites, to treat disease, to flavor food, and to beautify and pamper the body. When the Romans invaded England in the first century A.D., they took along their favorite herbs, like thyme and sage. Eventually, English physic gardens in monasteries, along with cottage gardens and still-rooms, were filled to overflowing with herbs and flowers used to treat illness or simply to make life more pleasant. Many of these medicinal flowering herbs originally came from China, where they continue to be used to this day. Beginning with Marco Polo in the thirteenth century, continuing with Portuguese traders in the sixteenth century, and finally through European and American plant fanciers in the 1800s, plants such as forsythia, hollyhock, and celosia made their way from East to West.

When the industrial revolution began luring people from a rural life to the cities, and man discovered how to chemically synthesize the curative properties of plants, the medicinal lore of many herbs was lost and they became simply ornamental additions to the garden. But the pendulum has swung back to an interest in herbal and natural medicines, especially traditional Chinese treatments, and once again we are beginning to realize how much more many familiar plants have to offer besides their beauty.

These herbs grow in our gardens, in fields, and along the roadside, ready to be plucked for a lovely bouquet. And savvy florist shops everywhere now offer such herbs as feverfew, tansy, Queen Anne's lace, bay, barberry, rosemary, and lavender, along with roses, peonies, hydrangea, and other herbal flowers. Add to these the leaves and berries of such herbal trees as silver birch, oak, and witch hazel, and it's easy to see how the idea of herbal bouquets has expanded from a simple tussy mussy carrying a message of love to colorful country bouquets, modern minimalist presentations, glorious wedding bouquets, and dramatic formal arrangements.

Ever eager to lure more people into the herb garden, Chris and I have written this book to show you the many ways herbs, both fresh and dried, can be used to create one-of-a-kind bouquets that will suffuse your home with color, fragrance, and beauty. So plant an herb garden, add more herbs to the border, and search the woods for inspiration—then make yourself a lovely herbal bouquet.

GATHERING

WHILE THE GARDEN MAY BE THE PRIMARY SOURCE

of material for your bouquets, the roadside, the open fields, and even the edges of the beach often offer interesting and beautiful herbs and "weeds." Flowering branches, berries, and interesting foliage, along with such charming flowers as milkweed, butterfly weed, chicory, Queen Anne's lace, wild roses, yarrow, bittersweet, soapwort, goldenrod, dame's rocket, and more are among the treasures you might find growing plentifully in the wild. Always carry a pair of clippers in your car, as many of the more inventive florists do: You never know when you might come upon an inspiring roadside treasure. However, be sure that you are not picking a protected plant (the list changes from state to state), and even when you're gathering something as prolific as wild yarrow, pick selectively and leave enough of the plant to ensure that it will continue to bloom the following year. And remember, too, that bits of bark, moss, twigs, birds' nests, seed pods, and even hornets' nests can be effective additions, especially to dried arrangements.

LEFT: A strict geometric plan contains the exuberant blooms of herbs and flowers in Eva Iooss's Long Island garden. "Organization is part of my Dutch blood," she says. Childhood memories of long rows of trees and straight canals through Holland's meadows inspired the simple, straight paths that delineate the sections. While allowing easy access for weeding and harvesting, they also enable her to indulge her sense of organization by caring for one bed a day.

Fields and woods can be filled with scratchy twigs and prickly thorns, so dress in long pants and a long-sleeved shirt as well as gloves to protect yourself when gathering in the wild. Add socks if you live in an area where ticks are a problem—and then be sure to take a shower and scrub well within twenty-four hours. Keep an eye out, too, for poison ivy or snakes if they are common in your area.

Your own garden will offer a more convenient source of flowers and foliage, but whether you go to the garden or farther afield in search of plant material, try to time your picking for early morning or the end of the day. The hot midday sun puts great stress on plants, particularly flowers, making them limp and less long-lived in your bouquet. Unless you are assembling a bouquet to be used that day, look for buds that are just beginning to open rather than full-blown flowers: They'll last longer. Use well-sharpened clippers to avoid tearing the edges of the stems. If possible, carry a bucket of barely warm water with you and plunge the flowers directly into the water as soon as you cut them to prevent the stem from "healing," which makes it more difficult for the flowers to drink.

As you pick, keep your bouquet in mind. Choose a variety of shapes and textures of flowers and foliage or masses of just one flower. Stick with a single hue, combine colors harmoniously, or dare to create a kaleidoscope mix. Make sure you have enough flowers and foliage for a lush bouquet or select just one exquisite bloom to display on its own. With so many choices, each sortie is a new chance to flex your creative muscles.

Barbara Bockbrader uses the flowers from her garden at Campo de' Fiori in the Berkshires to create vibrant bouquets for both clients and her own pleasure. LEFT: The meadow garden is filled with mullein, thistles, poppies, and other wild flowers. RIGHT: In the more traditional garden, a basket on a stick frees both hands for the pleasant task of gathering flowers.

a garden hat

Some pretty ribbon and a few dried flowers can transform an ordinary straw hat into an eye-catching chapeau. The effect can be simple or lush, depending on the types and numbers of flowers used. Wear this glorious flower-strewn hat for a special occasion or merely hang it decoratively on your wall.

materials

Straw hat

Ribbon (a piece long enough to encircle the crown of the hat)

Straight pins

Needle

Thread to match the ribbon

Dried flowers

Glue gun

Hair spray

❋ Choose a ribbon whose colors complement the flowers and whose width seems compatible with the hat. The slantier the crown of the hat, the narrower the ribbon will have to be.

❋ Wrap the ribbon around the crown of the hat, overlapping the ends slightly. Hold it in place with straight pins. Carefully tack the ribbon to the crown in several places to secure it and to hold the ends in place.

❋ Arrange the flowers on the brim. One by one, starting in the center and on the base layer next to the hat, glue the flowers in place. If necessary, hold them in place until the glue dries.

❋ Coat the flowers lightly with hair spray to protect them from reabsorbing moisture.

herbal flowers and foliage

From the sharply colored sprays of lady's mantle to the dramatic blue stalks of monkshood, there are herbal flowers suited to bouquets for every occasion and every taste. Herbal foliage, whether the twisting, berry-laden vines of bittersweet, the silvery gray cut leaves of mugwort, or the deep red leaves of purple basil, offers more choices for an amazing variety of color, texture, and shape. A true gem is the plant that offers both flowers and foliage: here are some of the best.

flowers

Allium	Cornflower	Joe-pye weed	Queen Anne's lace
Anise hyssop	Cow parsnip	Johnny-jump-ups	Roses
Bee balm	Dianthus	Lavender	Soapwort
Broom	Elecampane	Lobelia	Sunflower
Butterfly weed	Euphorbia	Loosestrife	Tansy
Calamintha	Feverfew	Mallow	Teasel
Calendula	Foxglove	Monkshood	Thistle
Catnip	Garlic chives	Meadow rue	Thyme
Chamomile	Goldenrod	Meadowsweet	Valerian
Chervil	Heather	Mullein	Vitex
Chives	Hollyhock	Pokeweed	Witch hazel
Clary sage	Hyssop	Poppies	Yarrow
Coneflower	Iris	Primrose	

foliage

Ambrosia	Castor oil plant	Lemon balm	Privet
Artemesias	Eucalyptus	Lemon leaves	Rosemary
Bamboo	Fig	Mugwort	Sassafrass
Barberry	Hemlock	Myrtle	Saw palmetto
Bay	Holly	Oak	Sea holly
Beech	Hops	Parsley	Southernwood
Birch	Horsetail	Peppers	Spruce
Bittersweet	Ivy	Pine	Wormwood
Boxwood	Juniper	Pomegranates	

flowers and foliage

Acanthus	Fennel	Nasturtium	Scented
Angelica	Germander	Peony	geraniums
Artichoke	Horehound	Rhubarb	Sweet cicely
Baptisia	Lady's mantle	Sages	Sweet woodruff
Basils	Lamb's ears	Salad burnet	Violet
Dill	Marjoram	Santolina	
Elder	Mints		

lavender linen spray

The sweetly pungent fragrance of lavender has been a favorite for scenting linens ever since the sixteenth century, when the lady of the house spread her sheets over lavender bushes to dry. Today, even without your own garden, you can enjoy this small luxury. Tuck small bunches of lavender or sachets among the sheets in your linen closet, add a few drops of lavender oil to the rinse water of your wash, or try spraying your dry sheets with this lavender water. The soothing fragrance will help you relax, and will ensure a pleasant sleep.

1 pint distilled water

1 tablespoon vodka

12 to 15 drops essential oil of lavender

Place the ingredients in a spray bottle and shake well. The vodka helps disperse the oil in the water. Spray on pillows and sheets after making the bed or before storing sheets in the linen closet.

CONDITIONING

WHEN YOU BUY FLOWERS, THE FLORIST HAS

already conditioned them to assure that your bouquet will last as long as possible. It's important to treat the flowers and foliage you pick just as carefully to get the maximum enjoyment and life from your bouquets.

As soon as you get the flowers inside, put them into a large container filled with cool to warm water. Make sure the container—and any vases you use later on—are absolutely clean; wash them with warm soapy water to which you've added a tablespoon or so of bleach to kill any lingering bacteria. Most flowers will be happy with cool to warm water, but there are exceptions: Hydrangeas and other woody stems like warm to hot water, and roses definitely like it hot. To mimic the glucose-making process that occurs in the garden, add commercial flower food to nourish the flowers and help the buds develop. If commercial food is unavailable, a combination of sugar and aspirin or a cup of lemon-lime soda is a good substitute. Don't overdo these additives, however, or you'll do more harm than good. The water should reach almost up to the blossom. Recut each stem at a 45-degree angle, then plunge it into the prepared water immediately. Again, make sure your clippers are very sharp so the cut is clean. By cutting at an angle, you'll expose a greater area of the inside of the stem to the water and you'll prevent the stems from sitting flat on the bottom of the container, thus hindering maximum water absorption. If the stem has nodes, make the cut between them to help the stem drink water more easily. Once all the flowers are in the large container, check for any damaged petals or wilted flowers and remove

LEFT: The parterre in front of Gail Shaw's Massachusetts house was inspired by the medieval cloistered gardens of France, where "chaos within order" was the norm. A profusion of miniature roses, feverfew, rose campion, and poppies are neatly framed by the gravel paths. Box and a quince tree, typically grown in such a garden, add structure.
BELOW: For an unpretentious country bouquet, mass feverfew in a white ironstone pitcher.

them. Mist the flowers and let them sit in a cool place for several hours or, if possible, place them in a cool, dark spot overnight before arranging the bouquet. This will make the stems stiffer and easier to handle.

Certain plants require special handling. Those with hollow stems, such as angelica and Queen Anne's lace, wilt more quickly unless they have water inside the length of the stems. Before plunging them into your water-filled container, fill the stem with water and cover the bottom with your finger to hold the water in. Woody stems should be split along their length for two or three inches to encourage drinking; if they are very thick and tough, smash the bottom few inches with a hammer instead. Any flowers that have a milky substance in the stem, such as poppies, hydrangeas, hollyhock, and sunflowers, must be seared quickly with a match or candle flame or dipped in boiling water for fifteen seconds to keep their vital fluids from oozing out.

When you bring roses in from the garden, remove the thorns with one of the special tools available for this chore or by running a sharp knife along the stems from top to bottom. Not only are the roses less dangerous to handle with no thorns, but they can also be eased in and out of the arrangement more easily. If they have been out of water for more than a few hours, submerge them completely in cool water for several hours to revive them. Whether you are dealing with garden roses or those from the florist, recut the stems, under water if possible, and get them into the water within seconds of recutting to prevent air bubbles from entering the stem and inhibiting the flower's ability to take up water.

flower teas

A simple cup of tea takes on a subtle complexity when fragrant herbal flowers and leaves are added to the brew. A touch of dried citrus peel augments the flavor even more.

¼ cup dried rose petals, lavender
blossoms, or mint leaves

2 cups loose orange pekoe tea

¼ cup dried orange or lemon peel
(optional)

Be sure that the herbs are completely dry before use, or they may mold in the jars. Mix all the ingredients thoroughly and store them in an airtight jar or tin. Use one teaspoonful of flavored tea for each cup of boiling water and brew as usual. Fresh petals and citrus rind may be used if you want to make smaller amounts of tea to use immediately.

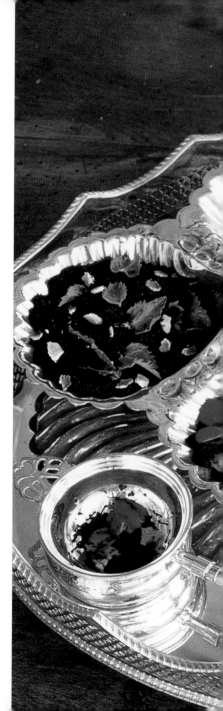

DRYING

IF YOU ARE PLANNING TO USE YOUR HERBS

for dried arrangements, it is best to pick them after the morning dew has evaporated. There are several methods for drying; the best one to use will depend on the flowers and foliage.

air-drying

This method is the easiest and works well for most herbal foliage and many smaller herb flowers, such as marjoram, lavender, anise hyssop, and lady's mantle. It is also excellent for lamb's ears, yarrow, peonies, and roses, as well as stalks of hollyhocks.

After picking the herbs, gather eight to ten stems together, tie them tightly with raffia, string, or a rubber band, and hang them upside down from a beam, a rack, or pegs in a warm, well-ventilated, dry spot, away from sunlight. An airy attic, for example, is an excellent spot. If necessary, use a dehumidifier to keep the air dry and speed up drying time. Try to keep your drying area at an even, warm temperature, as cool air causes the flowers to reabsorb moisture. Avoid putting fresh flowers too close to your drying herbs, as this introduces more humidity into the air. Since too much light and humidity causes the colors to fade, the faster the flowers dry, the better the color and condition. The more petals the flowers have, or

PRECEDING PAGE: Albert Morris skillfully combines spiky artichokes, rounded hydrangea, silvery artemesia, fluffy goldenrod, velvety celosia, purple marjoram, bold sunflowers, pale wheat, full-blown roses, fragrant lavender, and more herbs from field and garden in a dramatic display.
RIGHT: Generous amounts of air-dried roses in a range of colors create a voluptuous bouquet.

the thicker the foliage, the longer they will take to dry. Check the hanging herbs after a few days. Removing unnecessary foliage will shorten the drying time. They are ready when the leaves are crisp to the touch and the stems snap easily. Leave them in place or pack them loosely in tissue in well-marked boxes and store in a dark, dry spot. When properly handled, the dried material should last all through the winter.

glycerine

The best method of preserving beech, oak, and other branches and foliage is to treat them with glycerine, which keeps them supple and easy to work with. Some foliage, like peonies and fall-hued oaks, will retain its natural color; most others will change to a rich bronze, brown, burgundy, or black. Put a mixture of one part glycerine to two parts hot water three inches deep in the bottom of a container. Strip the lower leaves, hammer and/or split the ends of the branches, and set them in the mixture. Depending upon the plant, it will take anywhere from one week to one month or more for the leaves to absorb the glycerine and be ready for use. They are ready when they feel waxy. If you overprocess the leaves, small drops may form on the surface. Simply wipe them off. During this time, make sure to replenish the liquid periodically to keep it at the required level. Once the glycerine is absorbed, hang the treated branches upside down in bunches until they are needed. Large leaves such as those of a fig tree, or individual leaves to be used for framing or crafting can be preserved by totally immersing them in a glycerine bath for five or six days.

ABOVE RIGHT: A few wall pegs in a well-ventilated room are an ideal and decorative way to dry a few bunches of herbs. RIGHT: Sunflower heads can be air dried or dried in a very low oven if you open the door periodically to allow steam to escape. Wire them to thin dowels for bouquets or use them in wreaths.

silica gel

Although it isn't practical to dry entire stems in silica gel, you can dry individual specimen flowers. Blossoms treated this way look more like fresh flowers than air-dried herbs, and it is an especially good way to treat full-blown roses and peonies, individual hollyhock blossoms, lilies, and other larger, many-petaled blooms or more delicate flowers. They can then become focal points in your arrangement.

Silica gel, which can be reused many times, is available at craft stores and florists and is more efficient than other desiccants such as sand, borax, or cornstarch. Not a true gel but rather a fine powder, silica should be used with caution—it is important to wear a mask while working with it to prevent the dust from entering your lungs. Place one inch of silica gel in the bottom of a large box with a tight-fitting lid. Leave one inch of stem on each flower and place double flowers faceup, single flowers facedown on the drying medium, leaving space around the edges and between the flowers. Set stalks of flowers such as larkspur and foxglove on their sides. To avoid flattening blossoms,

gently spoon silica around the base until they are fully supported. Then slowly pour the silica gel over the blossom, covering it completely and making sure it sifts down between the petals of such flowers as roses. Cover the box tightly and check the flowers after two or three days. Simple flowers will probably be done; more complex blooms will take longer. The flowers are ready when the petals feel papery and dry to the touch. Gently brush aside the silica gel and lift the flowers out with a slotted spoon. Shake off as much of the silica gel as possible; use a soft paintbrush to remove any that remains. Delicate flowers such as pansies and hollyhock blossoms tend to reabsorb moisture easily, so spray them with a light coating of hair spray to help preserve them.

To use the flowers in an arrangement, grasp a piece of floral wire and the one-inch stem in one hand. Attach a piece of green floral tape to the wire just under the flower head and, holding the tape taut, turn the stem until it is covered. Store, tightly covered, in a dry, dark spot until needed. Single blossoms like those used on the hats on pages 16 and 17 can be stored in airtight containers. In either case, sprinkle a little silica gel in the box to absorb any stray moisture.

LEFT: Herbs such as yarrow, goldenrod, lamb's ears, chives, roses, and marjoram can be air dried successfully. Although a drying rack is the traditional place to hang herbs and flowers, you can also suspend them from wall pegs, ceiling beams and racks, wooden frames backed with chicken wire, or even a wire hanger.

a pressed-flower bouquet

A two-dimensional pressed herbal bouquet is as enjoyable as one that comes fresh from the garden and will last much longer. The arrangement can be as simple or as complex as you choose. A single stem, as in the pages of an old herbarium, or a graphic display of a single lady's mantle leaf, especially when part of a similar grouping, is just as eye-catching as a collage of many-petaled roses and the lacy leaves of sweet cicely.

materials

Blotter paper and/or plain newsprint

Corrugated cardboard

A flower press or some heavy books

A selection of herbal flowers and leaves

Paper for backing

A small brush

Tweezers (optional)

White glue

❋ Cut the blotter paper, newsprint, and cardboard to the size of the press or the books.

❋ Pick flowers and leaves, preferably those that are relatively flat, when they are at their peak. Brown spots and wilted leaves or flowers do not improve with pressing. In picking the material and arranging it, think about texture, shape, and color just as you would in composing a fresh bouquet.

❋ Prepare your materials for pressing: many-petaled flowers can often be plucked judiciously to make them flatter; other flowers can be gently flattened out with your fingers. It may be necessary to dry stems and flowers separately.

❋ Place a piece of cardboard on the bottom of the press or on a book and add several layers of newsprint. If you are drying particularly moist specimens, put a piece of blotter paper over the newsprint. The newsprint acts as padding between layers and is adequate on its own for drying most specimens.

❋ Arrange the plant material on the paper, making sure no leaves are touching. If necessary, remove leaves or bend stems for a better line. Cover with another piece of blotting paper and/or a layer of newsprint and then another piece of cardboard. Repeat layers. Top with a final piece of cardboard and the top of the flower press or several heavy books.

❋ Check the specimens within twenty-four hours to make sure they are arranged as you wish. Minor changes can be made before the plants dry. After two weeks, remove those that are completely dry and store them, between layers of wax paper, in an airtight container. Allow any that are not completely dry to remain in the press for another week.

❋ Compose your bouquet on paper of your choice. Using a small brush and tweezers if necessary, apply glue piece by piece and press the plant material into place. Allow it to dry thoroughly.

❋ Frame the arrangement, allowing enough room between the backing and the glass so the flowers aren't crushed. Do not hang the "bouquet" in sunlight or the flowers will fade.

LEFT: Meadow rue, growing up three feet, is one of summer's tallest flowering herbs. RIGHT: A generous bunch of lavender makes a charming country bouquet in any container, but gains added sophistication when displayed in a colorful Oriental jug. Assemble the bunch before drying when the stems are still pliable.

microwave

Single flowers, sprigs of foliage, and single leaves can be dried in the microwave. This method, a variation on drying with silica gel, requires patience as it will involve a lot of trial and error. Microwave ovens vary greatly and so do the moisture content and drying times of various flowers, and although a microwave is very fast, only a limited number of flowers can be dried at one time.

Since each flower or leaf has its own drying time, work with only one type of flower or leaf at a time. Prepare a microwave-safe container with a one-inch layer of silica gel on the bottom. Cut the stem of each flower, leaving one inch of stem below the head, and set the flower upright in the silica gel. Continue to add silica gel around the flower head as described in the drying method on pages 35 to 37, making sure there is an inch of silica on top of the flowers. Set the uncovered container in the microwave on a rack. The amount of time it will take for the drying process will depend upon the number of flowers you are drying, the amount of silica gel being used, and on the flower itself. Generally speaking, a half pound of silica gel will require about two minutes; two pounds, about five minutes; and three and a half pounds, around six minutes. Always use your microwave at half power. Once the "cooking" time is over, flowers, like food, need a standing time ranging from ten minutes for simple flowers and leaves up to a half hour for more complex blooms. While the flowers are standing, cover the container, leaving just a crack, to prevent the contents from reabsorbing any moisture. Carefully remove the flowers: If any stems or flowers still contain moisture, cover that part of the flower again and return to the microwave briefly.

It's possible to take some of the guesswork out of this drying process by checking the temperature of the silica gel with an instant thermometer. Remove the container from the oven and insert the thermometer into the middle of the silica between flowers. Simple blossoms like the California poppy should be done when the silica reaches a temperature of 140°F. The more complex the flower, the higher the needed temperature will be, with multipetaled blooms like a rose or joe-pye weed requiring a temperature of 170°F. Always keep notes on the temperatures and times it takes to dry your flowers: This will make future drying sessions easier.

note on hydrangeas

The proper way to dry hydrangeas is a matter of much discussion. To begin with, picking the flowers at the right time is of prime importance: The flower heads should be firm to the touch, not soft or dry. If they are picked before the petals begin hardening off, the flowers simply tend to shrivel, although they can be dried successfully in silica gel. It is possible to hang hydrangeas upside down or set them in containers in a warm, dry, dark place until they dry. However, the most effective way to preserve their glorious blooms is to set the stems in an inch or two of water and allow them to absorb a little moisture during the drying process. They seem to retain color better with this method. Whichever method you choose, keep them away from sunlight and humidity.

A BOUQUET
OF FAVORITES

sprig of mint or basil, the lacy sprays of lady's mantle, the strong heads of yarrow, or the more voluptuous blooms of the rose, herbs provide a wonderful array of flowers. Many of the more striking and colorful of these blooms are best known as perennials with little thought of their herbal roots. Here is a rundown of our favorites of these often unacknowledged herbal bloomers. All will add color and drama to gardens and bouquets.

DAYLILY *(hemerocallis)*

Whether planted in great drifts or in smaller clumps in a border, the green foliage and colorful blossoms of daylilies are attractive additions to both garden and bouquet. As their name suggests, each flower lasts for just one day, but since there are numerous buds on each stem they bloom over a long period, even when cut. By choosing cultivars that flower early, mid-season, or late in the season you can have lilies in bloom the entire summer.

The Chinese originally cultivated daylilies for their delicate flavor. The buds, fresh or dried, are still tasty additions to soups, meats, and pasta; the flowers can be stuffed with fish salads or other delicate fillings. But the Chinese also respected daylilies for their medicinal properties, brewing a pleasant spring tonic from the fresh buds and drying extras for winter use. The resulting brew was thought to relieve pain, cure kidney problems, and ease sorrow by causing a loss of memory. The green leaves were fashioned into a poultice to treat burns.

These sturdy plants traveled west over the silk route with the spice caravans, finally arriving in England in the late sixteenth century. The Dutch brought daylilies to Manhattan. By the late 1800s, however, interest in daylilies waned, not to be rekindled until endless hybridization by professionals and amateurs alike produced thousands of cultivars. There are now more than 30,000, with flowers ranging from white through all stages of yellow, pink, orange, and red to maroon and multicolored varieties. Heights vary from the foot-tall dwarf varieties to three or four feet. The two daylilies favored by herbalists are *H. fulva* (orange), which flowers in July and August, and *H. lilioasphodelus* (yellow), flowering in May and June.

Generally hardy in zones 3 to 10, daylilies are easy to grow. Although a few of the paler varieties hold their color better with a little shade, most are happier and bloom more freely in full sun. Plant them in moist but well-drained soil and feed them with a light liquid fertilizer several times during the growing season. Too much nitrogen will weaken the stems.

To keep the plants vigorous and flowering copiously, divide the clumps every three to five years, preferably in the spring. Lift the roots carefully and gently pull them apart. Replant each division in a hole large enough to comfortably accommodate the roots. Make a cone of soil in the bottom of the hole and spread the roots over it, then work the remaining soil around the roots. Be sure the crown is no more than one inch below ground level. Space taller cultivars about two and a half feet apart; smaller plants from eighteen to twenty-four inches.

RIGHT: Landscape designer David Adams uses foxgloves as exclamation points in a border in his own Long Island garden. By allowing them to self-seed within limits, he gives the traditional beds a more casual air. A conical evergreen and roses grown on a tuteur add height, structure, and visual interest.

The stately spires of foxgloves add an architectural element where needed, turning the most ordinary planting into a spectacular display. A staple of cottage gardens, foxgloves are equally at home in an informal border, and quite happy in partial shade, they add their charm to woodland gardens, too. Ranging in height from two to six feet, in early to midsummer the colorful spikes bear flowers that open from the bottom up in shades of white, pink, mauve, yellow, and apricot. Many are biennial, flowering the second year; others are short-lived or true perennials. Once planted, they do not always behave as promised, however, reacting as they please to the soil and climate, fading away in some locations and reseeding profusely in others.

Outside the garden the plant is best known as the source of digitalis, an important heart medication derived from the dried leaves. Herbal healers treated heart problems with foxglove for many years before doctors isolated the healing properties and standardized dosages. Although foxglove may save lives when administered properly, the plant is highly toxic if eaten.

Among the twenty-two species of foxglove, the most common is *D. purpurea,* a short-lived perennial, which grows up to six feet tall and self-sows readily. Its white, pink, and purple flowers, spotted inside, grow on one side of the flower stalk. If you live in a warmer climate, this is the one to grow. It has spawned many hybrids, including the two-foot Foxy, which flowers after only

five months and can be grown as an annual, and it is one of the best fox-gloves for container growing. The individual flowers of Excelsior hybrids are held at right angles rather than drooping toward the ground and grow all around the spikes for more voluptuous blooms. Of all the species, they are the longest lasting in bouquets. To prolong the life of cut foxgloves, pick them when the flowers are only half open.

D. x mertonensis, another short-lived perennial, has shiny deep-green foliage instead of the woolly leaves of *D. purpurea;* its flowers grow all around the stalk. *D. lanata* (Grecian foxglove) is a true perennial and blooms later in the summer than the others. The two-foot spikes have pale cream flowers spotted with violet brown. *D. lutea* and *D. gran-diflora* are also perennials with yellow flowers on two-foot stems.

Foxgloves are easy to grow in zones 4 to 8. Almost any soil will do, if the plants are watered regularly, but mixing in organic material gives even better results. While they prefer a bit of shade in warm climates, in cooler locations they can withstand full sun. In warm climates sow seeds directly in the garden in the fall, or in cooler ones in May or June. For an earlier start, plant the seeds in a cold frame in early spring. Mix the tiny seeds with sand before sowing to distribute them more evenly. The seeds must be left uncovered to germinate. When seedlings are about five inches tall, plant them where they can grow undisturbed during the summer, then transfer them in the fall to their permanent home, where they'll be ready to bloom the following summer. After flowering, let the seed heads dry and then bend the stem down toward the ground. This gets the seeds closer to the earth, increasing the chances of reseeding and neatens up the garden at the same time. If you want foxgloves else-where in the garden, cut the stalk off and shake the seed heads wherever you hope for new plants.

rose-petal jelly

This exotically sweet jelly is lovely with brown bread spread with butter or cream cheese or as a filling for cookies and cakes. For maximum flavor use very fragrant roses, preferably red or deep pink.

1 cup fresh organically grown rose petals, white heel removed

2 cups water

4 cups sugar

¼ cup cider vinegar

3 ounces liquid pectin

½ cup chopped fresh organically grown rose petals, white heel removed

Place the rose petals in a mixing bowl. Bring the water to a boil and pour it over the petals. Steep, covered, until cool. Strain the infusion into another bowl, pressing all the liquid out of the petals to get the most flavor. In a nonaluminum saucepan, combine 2 cups of the rose infusion with the sugar and vinegar. Bring to a boil over high heat, and as soon as the sugar has dissolved, stir in the pectin. Return the mixture to a rolling boil, stirring, and boil for exactly one minute. Remove the pan from the heat and skim any foam from the top of the jelly.

Stir the chopped petals into the jelly and pour it into sterilized jars. If the petals do not stay suspended, stir occasionally with a sterilized utensil until the jelly thickens enough to hold them in place. Seal with a thin layer of paraffin. If you do not intend to use the jelly within a month or two, use canning jars, omit the paraffin, and process the jelly in a hot-water bath according to the jar manufacturer's instructions.

Makes 5 to 6 half-pint jars

GOLDENROD *(Solidago)*

In late summer and early autumn, masses of bright yellow goldenrod brighten fields and country roadsides. The blooming season seems to extend for weeks. That's because there are generally several of the 100 or so varieties of this plant growing side by side, their flowers displayed in erect spikes or falling in graceful racemes. Once respected for healing wounds, this herb is now often regarded as a weed and shunned because of an erroneous belief that it's the source of hay fever (when actually the simultaneously blooming ragweed is the culprit). Over the years, many English gardeners have used less hardy hybrids like the dwarf Golden Baby or Goldenmosa to perk up late summer borders. Goldenrod's bold burst of color is also welcomed by ecological gardeners, who rely on native plants that thrive without excessive water or pesticides. The flowers, both fresh and dried, are a splendid addition to country bouquets. Pick goldenrod when the flowers are half open, especially for drying: Fully open blooms turn to fluff when dried.

Goldenrod is easy to grow in zones 5 to 9 and thrives in well-drained, average to poor soil as long as it has plenty of sun. Because the plants are so robust, look for the above-named hybrids, such as Golden Baby, which are less invasive and more colorful and have slightly larger flowers. Site the plants carefully to avoid overwhelming less vigorous plants, and remove the flower heads before they go to seed to keep this prolific herb under control. Buy plants or sow seeds in the spring; propagate mature plants by division in either spring or fall.

HOLLYHOCK *(Althea rosea)*

With their old-fashioned charm, hollyhocks engender thoughts of country gardens. Beginning in midsummer, the buds on the stately stalks begin to flower, gradually opening the length of the stem from bottom to top. With proper care, they will continue to put forth an occasional blossom until early autumn.

As familiar as hollyhocks are today, their history is more exotic than you might expect. In ancient China the flowers were cultivated as a beautiful ornamental, and the cooked leaves were considered a tasty spring green, the flower buds a delicacy. The Romans, too, often enjoyed hollyhocks at the table. Over the years the hollyhock has been used medicinally for everything from calming coughs to soothing insect bites. Indeed, the word *althea* is Greek for "that which heals."

By the Renaissance, the hollyhock had become a favorite in England's cottage gardens, and in 1631 English settlers brought the seeds to New England. Soon, hollyhocks were growing all across the country as pioneers scattered seeds wherever they settled. Stands of these old farmhouse hollyhocks can still be found growing happily beside old houses and barns. Even Thomas Jefferson was captivated

by the exotic "black" hollyhock *(A. nigra),* which he grew at Monticello.

There are sixty species of biennial and short-lived perennial holly-hocks. Once established, however, the biennials self-seed so prolifically that they can be counted on to return year after year. In fact, you will have to thin out the volunteers that pop up around the garden. Each plant produces multiple stems of flowers that soar as high as eight feet above a dense clump of large, rounded leaves. The spires are covered with blossoms, either single or double, ranging in color from white and pale pinks, yellows, and apricot to red, deep pink, and a maroon so dark it is referred to as "black." Seeds may be sown directly in the garden in August, and if well protected, these seedlings may flower the following year, although they may not reach their full height. Seeds may also be started indoors in early winter or sown in the garden as soon as the soil warms up, but don't count on flowers for another year. Plant seedlings or plants from the nursery about two feet apart to allow good air circulation and discourage rust and mildew. Once you have an established clump, you can collect the seed heads when they begin to open, dry them completely, and store them in a dark, dry place until you're ready to start your seedlings. Or immediately scatter the seed heads in the garden where you want more hollyhocks.

These imposing plants grow well in zones 3 to 9, but it's best to plant them against a house or wall to give them some protection from strong winds. Even in a protected spot, however, they might need staking because of their height. For best results, plant them in good, well-drained soil in full sun. Thankfully, hollyhocks are a hardy lot, and once entrenched they will sustain a certain amount of neglect and drought.

From midsummer through early fall, hydrangea's large flowers, actually clusters of small florets, are set off against the glossy dark leaves. Hydrangea is a native of North America; the roots and bark were once used by Native Americans as a diuretic, a role that herbalists still give *H. arborescens.* Today, however, hydrangeas are best known for their decorative qualities. Hydrangeas perform well as a fresh-cut flower when properly conditioned, and they also dry beautifully to be enjoyed throughout the winter.

The showy bushes of *H. macrophylla,* the most popular species, grow from three to six feet tall and as wide—or wider—making them especially useful to fill large spaces or as an informal hedge. Kept under control, they are handsome additions to the border. Though they prefer full sun, hydrangeas also grow quite happily in partial shade, so they are an excellent choice to plant at the edge of a natural woodland site.

The two best-known cultivars of *H. macrophylla* are the Lace-Caps with their flat, open flower heads of tiny florets surrounded by an edging of larger ones; and the Hortensias, often referred to as mopheads because of their big, spherical flowers. These flowers range from white through all shades of blue, from pale to cobalt, to various pinks and purples. The colors, except for white, may be altered by changing the acidity of the soil. To turn them bluer, add aluminum sulfate to the soil in the springtime before blooming starts; add lime to make them pinker.

Plant hydrangeas in moist, but well-drained, fairly rich soil where they are, if possible, sheltered from cold winds. Hardy to zone 6, they can suffer during severe winters if they are not protected. Dig a hole that is twice the size of the rootball and put a one-inch layer of compost in the bottom. After loosening the soil around the roots, set the hydrangea in the hole with the base of the stems at ground level, adding more soil if necessary. Shovel the remaining soil around the roots, water thoroughly, and mulch with more compost. For the lushest flowers, keep the plants well watered and fertilize them in the spring. Once the plants are established, you can propagate hydrangeas from cuttings of soft wood in early summer or of hard wood in the winter, or by layering young stems during the summer.

Flowers are produced on previous years' growth, so prune the shrubs in early spring before new growth starts. To make room for new shoots, cut one quarter of the oldest stems, including damaged branches and dead wood, back to the ground, then prune the remaining flowering stems at the first bud or pair of buds below the flower. Leave new shoots from the past summer untouched.

NASTURTIUM (Tropaeolum)

From spring until fall, brightly colored nasturtiums climb over trellises and walls, edge borders, or tumble down hillsides, adding a cheery note to the

RIGHT: Albert Morris plants nasturtiums in large pots on a pool deck. Dwarf and semidwarf varieties are useful for underplanting larger herbs or trees. NEXT PAGE: At Merriment Gardens in Sussex, England, trailing nasturtiums twine through a rustic bench.

garden. This Peruvian native was taken back to Spain by the conquistadores in the sixteenth century. From there, nasturtiums traveled to England and eventually to the rest of Europe.

Since the earliest days, nasturtiums have been grown for their vitamin-laden leaves, a peppery substitute for watercress, to which they are related. The leaves are delicious in salads and sandwiches; so are the funnel-shaped flowers, which can also be a spicy addition to vinegar and an enticing hors d'oeuvre when stuffed with herbed cheese, crabmeat, or other tasty fillings. Nasturtiums, once a part of the home pharmacy, are no longer used medicinally, but the leaves remain a potent source of vitamin C, especially before flowering starts.

There are eighty to ninety species of nasturtiums that climb, trail along the ground, or form bushy little plants. Although a few grow from tuberous roots, those most commonly seen in the garden are cultivars of *T. majus.* The bright-green kidney-shaped leaves, sometimes as big as seven inches across, provide a wonderful backdrop for flowers ranging from rich cream and apricot through bright yellow, orange, red, and a deep mahogany. While the climbing and trailing varieties may grow to ten feet, the bushy cultivars, including dwarf and double-flowered varieties, are only one to two feet tall, making them excellent choices for window boxes, containers, and borders.

Perennial in warm climates, nasturtiums grow as annuals in cooler areas. Sow the seeds one-half to three-quarters of an inch deep as soon as the soil warms up in early spring. Since they do not take well to transplanting, sow the seeds where they are to grow. Thin the seedlings to six to nine inches apart. Although nasturtiums prefer sandy, moderately rich soil, they will do well almost anywhere with enough sun and water. Too much fertilizer produces more foliage at the expense of flowers.

a bouquet salad

When you lace even the most ordinary lettuces with a bouquet of fresh herbs and flowers, a salad assumes an amazing sensory sophistication. As your palate encounters the refreshing tang of mint among the subtle lettuces, followed by the anise essence of a fennel sprig or the peppery tang of a nasturtium leaf or flower, it should be stimulated, mystified, and amused by one marvelous flavor at a time. Use only the tender tips of the leafy herbs (or single leaves if they are bigger) and perfect flowers, and practice restraint for a subtle effect.

4 cups assorted greens

4 chives or garlic chives, cut into 2-inch pieces

4 sprigs of mint

4 sprigs of salad burnet

4 sprigs of fennel

4 sprigs of marjoram

Edible flowers such as nasturtium, hyssop, and thyme

Vinaigrette of your choice

Wash and dry the greens, herbs, and flowers. Place the greens in a bowl with the herb sprigs and flowers on top. Just before serving, add the vinaigrette and toss well to distribute the sprigs.

Serves 4

PEONY *(Paeonia)*

One of the showiest of herbal flowers, the peony is also one of the earliest to appear in the garden. From late spring through early summer, the early, mid-, and late varieties, most of them cultivars of *P. lactiflora,* produce large, colorful, and sometimes fragrant blossoms above handsome dissected leaves.

The peony was once widely respected for its medicinal value as well as for its beauty. While Chinese doctors still employ the root, elsewhere the peony is now loved solely for its glorious flowers and subtle perfume. These flowers range from simple single blossoms to full rounded spheres resembling a rose, and they come in a stunning range of whites, pinks, and red as well as the occasional coral and yellow. Though they are at their most gorgeous straight from the garden, they can also be air-dried for winter bouquets. Whether you plan to put them in a fresh bouquet or to dry them, for best results pick the flowers just as they open.

Peonies are extremely long-lived perennials that grow on a thick, knotted rootstock. There are reports of clumps that are still vigorous after 100 years. While the root may be divided in the fall, once the plant is established, it should be left undisturbed. It's wise, therefore, to prepare the ground well before planting. Dig an eighteen-inch-deep hole, cover the bottom with composted manure, then fill it partway with a mixture of topsoil and compost to which you've added a cup of bonemeal. Plant the root eye-side up so that no more than one to two inches of soil covers the eyes, planting the eyes too deep hinders the flowering mechanism. Since peonies, viable in zones 3 through 7 or 8, bloom better when exposed to cold weather, the warmer the climate, the closer the root should be to ground level. Space the plants about three feet apart in well-drained soil, preferably where they are protected from strong winds and away from the greedy roots of trees and shrubs. Work the soil around the roots and water them in well. Although they prefer full sun, peonies will get along with some shade but may not bloom as profusely.

Always look for roots that have at least three and preferably five eyes: Each will produce a stem. It will take three years for the plants to reach maturity, but then you will have lush bushes up to three feet tall covered with flowers. Although some stems produce only a single flower, others may have many side shoots. If you want blooms worthy of a flower show, snip the secondary buds off so that all the energy can go into the central flower. Peonies are often too heavy for their stems, especially after a rainstorm, and need support. Otherwise, these rewarding plants require little care except for extra watering during dry spells and a boost of fertilizer in the spring and again after blooming.

For centuries the poppy has been grown for its beauty as well as its therapeutic capabilities. The Egyptians included these colorful flowers in graves to assure life after death, while early Romans believed the juice of the plant could ease the pains of love. While the opium poppy *(P. somniferum)* is the source of many drug problems (and can't be grown commercially for that reason), it is also the source of morphine, a staple of modern medicine. The more benign corn poppy *(P. rhoeas),* which contains no opium, serves as a sedative and cough suppressant that is mild enough even for children. More practically, it is used to color medicines, wine, and ink and as a mild skin freshener.

There are dozens of papaver species, ranging from the bright red corn poppy that grows wild in the fields from early to late summer to the majestic Oriental poppy *(P. orientale)* with its flamboyant flowers atop thick, hairy stems that sometimes reach four feet in the air. Most are annuals or biennials treated as annuals and reseed profusely.

Hybrids of the Iceland poppy *(P. nudicaule),* the opium poppy, and the corn poppy are the most popular garden choices and generally are treated as annuals. All boast silky single, double, or fringed flowers in bright to pastel shades of pink, white, orange, red, and yellow. They are generally carried on single stems that sway, depending on variety, from one to four feet above handsomely cut foliage. The true perennial Oriental poppy, viable in zones 3 to 7, has striking saucer-shaped flowers sometimes as wide as twelve inches across. These large blossoms, in shades of red, orange, salmon, white, or pink, often have black spots in the center, heightening the drama.

All poppies make splendid if short-lived additions to a bouquet. To prolong their life, pick the buds just before they shed their hairy

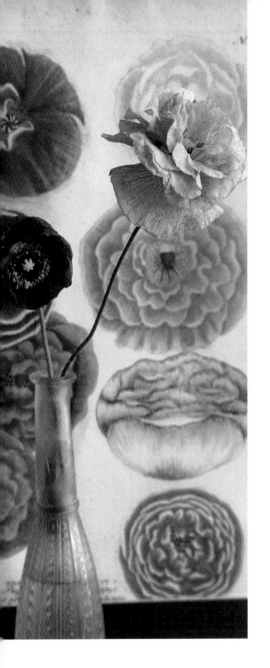

covering, preferably in the evening. Immediately sear the stems with a match or dip them in boiling water for fifteen seconds to prevent the life-giving milky sap from draining out, then plunge the flowers in water up to their necks until morning. When dried, the seed heads are an interesting accent to dried arrangements, while the mild, nutty flavor of the seeds, particularly those of the bread poppy *(P. somniferum)*, are a favorite of bakers, who stir them into everything from bagels to pound cakes. When ripe, the seeds contain no opium.

In general, annual poppies like full sun and good, well-drained, alkaline soil. In cooler areas, mix the seeds with four parts sand and scratch them into the soil just before freezing or in early spring. In hot climates, sow seeds in the fall for early spring blooms. Always sow them in place, as they do not take well to transplanting.

Oriental poppies should be started from seed planted indoors in the spring, then transplanted to a sunny part of the garden in late summer when the plant is dormant. In humus-rich soil they will eventually form large clumps that can provide root cuttings for propagation in late summer or be divided in the spring. Since the foliage dies down after flowering, plant Oriental poppies at the back of the border or among later flowering perennials to camouflage the empty space.

lemon poppy seed cake

Wonderful on its own with a cup of tea, this cake is also a perfect accompaniment to fruits and ice cream.

1 cup (2 sticks) butter, softened

2 cups sugar

6 eggs, separated

3 cups sifted all-purpose flour

1 teaspoon baking soda

½ teaspoon salt

⅓ cup poppy seeds

Juice and grated zest of 1 lemon

1 cup sour cream

lemon glaze

½ cup fresh lemon juice

1 pound (1 box) confectioners' sugar, sifted

Preheat the oven to 350°F. Grease and flour a 10-inch springform tube pan and set it aside. In a large bowl, cream the butter. Gradually add 1½ cups of the sugar and continue to beat until the mixture is light and fluffy. Beat in the egg yolks one at a time.

Combine the flour, baking soda, and salt. Stir the poppy seeds, the lemon juice, and the zest into the sour cream. Add the dry ingredients to the butter mixture, alternating with the sour cream.

In another bowl, beat the egg whites until they hold soft peaks. Gradually beat in the remaining ½ cup of sugar, beating until the whites are glossy and hold their shape. Gently fold one third of the whites into the batter. Fold in the remaining whites, the lemon juice, and the zest. Pour the batter into the pan. Bake for 55 to 60 minutes, or until a cake tester inserted in the cake comes out clean. Cool the cake on a rack for 5 minutes, then gently run a knife around the sides and remove the outer ring. Loosen the cake from the tube and the bottom, turn it out, and invert it onto a rack right-side up. Cool.

For the glaze, stir enough lemon juice into the sugar to make a thin glaze. Spoon the glaze over the cake.

Serves 10 to 12

CONTAINERS

WHEN ARRANGING A BOUQUET, YOUR CHOICE

of container is just as important as the flowers. The right container can enhance the feeling you want to create as well as add a sense of individuality to the bouquet. A mixed arrangement, for example, takes on a more formal look in an urn than in a basket; a few stems of poppies make a more distinctive centerpiece when each is placed in an individual bottle than if the lot were simply grouped in a small vase.

Although anything from an old teapot to a watering can can serve as a vase, choosing the right container will make your bouquets truly unique. Collect a supply of unusual pieces in which to display your arrangements, and be creative in choosing the container you want to use. Here are a few tips for making the perfect container selection.

LEFT: Flea markets, yard sales, the kitchen cupboard, even the garden shed can yield unusual vases. Pretty pitchers, graceful bowls, celery holders, footbaths, pails, watering cans, old bottles, and even small glasses make interesting containers for everything from a tiny nosegay to a major floral display.

* The location where your finished bouquet will rest will influence the bouquet and container. What type of bouquet will look best there: tall and narrow, rounded, pyramid shape, low and wide? The container should reflect the shape of the bouquet and be of a comparable size.

* Decide whether you want a formal or informal feeling. Remember, however, that sometimes the juxtaposition of an informal container against a formal setting can be very effective.

* Consider the colors of the room and the flowers, and choose a container that complements them.

Once you've determined the general size, shape, color, and feeling needed, there is an endless variety of containers from which to choose. You needn't limit yourself to traditional vases, but ideally you should have a basic collection of classic shapes: a sphere, a cylinder, a trumpet, a square, a low pan, a pail, and a bottle shape.

Be creative and look at everything in your cupboards with the idea of using it to hold flowers: silver cups, ice buckets, chamber pots, tureens, bowls, bottles, pitchers, even vintage jelly and canning jars or old egg cups can be pressed into service. Don't let holes or cracks discourage you: Items such as a ceramic strainer, a cheese mold, a basket, or a cracked pitcher can be fitted with a glass or plastic container to keep the water from escaping. Carefully coating the inside of a crack with silicone also makes a damaged container waterproof.

Nature provides more choices. Bamboo stems and shells make handsome containers, as do hollowed-out fruits and vegetables such as pumpkins, lemons, and artichokes. There are also many different sizes, shapes, and colors of gourds that can be dried and used naturally or painted and polished. The latter are not waterproof, so limit them to dried arrangements or set a waterproof container inside.

Let a thoughtful use of containers make up for a lack of flowers. If you find an inexpensive container in a simple classic shape, buy multiples and tuck a single stalk in each for an impressive display. Use tiny bottles, cups, or vases for a little nosegay to set at an individual place setting, on a bedside or bathroom table, or on a desk.

PRECEDING PAGE: Humble country bouquets of herbs and garden flowers show to great advantage in a collection of blue-and-white enamelware pitchers, pails, and teapots. RIGHT: An antique patterned ironstone pitcher adds a touch of elegance to a casual mix of pastel and golden yarrows, lamb's ears, marjoram, roses, and other herbs.

an herbal vase

In the case of bamboo and angelica, the herb itself can be used as a container for your bouquets. These plants have natural partitions at intervals along the stem, which act as the bottom of the "vase," although with angelica the membrane must be reinforced with silicone to make it waterproof.

Angelica stems

Silicone (optional)

Polyurethane (optional)

Glue gun

Raffia

Moss

At the end of the season, cut large dried angelica stems ½ inch below the lowest section. Cut the stems in varying lengths, always cutting ½ inch below a section.

If you plan to use the "vase" for fresh flowers, fill the section at the bottom of the stem with silicone and allow it to dry. Alternatively, when arranging the bouquet, you can set glass tubes of water in the larger stems; put the flowers in florist's tubes in the smaller ones. Dried flowers will require no special preparation. If desired, polyurethane the stems for a shiny finish.

Assemble an uneven number of stems in various heights and sizes into an interesting design. Using a glue gun, attach the stems to each other. Work piece by piece, using adequate glue to solidly adhere the pieces. Hold them together manually until the glue dries. Wrap the finished vase with a generous band of raffia, set it on a base, and surround it with moss.

ARRANGING

FLOWERS ADD COLOR
AND WARMTH TO ANY

room, and perhaps more importantly they bring pleasure to the beholder. With a little practice anyone can arrange herbs and flowers into an appealing bouquet, whether it's a handful of flowers dropped casually into a pitcher, a bunch of chive blossoms in a kitchen crock, or a more structured arrangement in a silver urn. Even a single flower in a handsome vintage bottle can be satisfying. As long as the result pleases you, it will generally please others, too.

The first step in planning a bouquet is to decide where it will be displayed and the size and shape best suited to that spot. Scale is all-important. A tiny arrangement, no matter how beautiful, will look ridiculous on a large buffet, just as an enormous arrangement would be out of place in a small bathroom or on a night table. Consider the shape, too. Would a short and rounded bouquet or a tall, linear one be more appropriate? A centerpiece should be low enough to see and talk over, but it could be round, square, or rectangular depending in part on the shape of the table. A tall, imposing bouquet, on the other hand, would be more suitable for an entryway or a buffet.

After selecting an appropriate container whose size, shape, and color complement the spot and the room, choose your plant materials. Bouquets may be

PRECEDING PAGE: A subtly hued mixture of lamb's ears, lady's mantle, Irish bells, and pale roses are mounded in a simple glass flute set on the windowsill at Blantyre. RIGHT: A stroll through the garden yielded such herbs as catmint, roses, cosmos, buddleia, sage, garlic chives, and phlox to fashion this predominantly pink and purple country bouquet, which is set off handsomely by the blue ceramic vase.

composed of flowers of all one size or different sizes. You might want to limit the arrangement to all one kind of flower—a grouping of peonies, for example, is a splendid sight—or combine different but similarly shaped flowers such as roses, peonies, and hydrangeas for a lush effect. For a more visually striking bouquet, mix rounded shapes with sharper edges and spikes; contrast textures such as the downy leaves of lamb's ears or sage against shiny leaves of boxwood or bay, the puckered leaves of mint, or the spikiness of lavender or rosemary. Use bold leaves like those of the castor bean plant or the fig tree, the fern-like leaves of sweet cicely and yarrow, the jagged foliage of lady's mantle and thistle, and the architectural forms of horsetail and bamboo, or mix in the varied shapes and rich colors of fruits and vegetables for added drama.

In any bouquet, color choices are equally flexible. Although it's possible to choose the specific colors you want to use when ordering an arrangement from a florist, bouquets picked from the garden will depend on what's available. Monochromatic arrangements, whether composed of one type of flower or a mixture of many varieties, are always safe and can be stunning. Almost as foolproof is a harmonious mix of related colors like pinks and purples. A clash of all the colors in the garden can be exciting to behold but is also a bit more difficult to handle. In nature the most unlikely colors seem to work together; they will in a bouquet, too, if you keep the colors in balance just as you would in a border. However, it is important to remember where the flowers will be placed and to be sure the colors are in sync with their surroundings.

Once you've determined the size and shape of the bouquet and selected the flowers and container, you must decide how to anchor the bouquet in the container. There are several tried-and-true methods. Experiment until you find the one that works best for you. Perhaps the

most natural foundation is made by crossing six strong stems in the container to form a framework to hold the remaining flowers. This will produce a very natural look, but it is a difficult way to work if you want a highly stylized bouquet. Old-fashioned frogs, available in a variety of sizes and shapes, also work well for simple bouquets. For larger, more complex arrangements, work with florist's foam or chicken wire. There are several brands of florist's foam; the professional-quality foam, which has many holes in it, allows the flowers to absorb water more easily.

First, cut the foam to fit the container. A large bowl might require several pieces. If so, for a really secure foundation, encase them in a piece of chicken wire to hold them in place. Soak the foam in hot water containing floral food for at least thirty minutes before using. Alternatively, omit the foam and insert a ball of crumpled chicken wire of an appropriate size in the container. Either way, if you are planning a major bouquet, the foundation will be sturdier if you make a grid of green florist's tape over the top of the container. (For a simple arrangement, the grid itself might be enough of a foundation.) If you do use tape, remember the bouquet will have to droop over the edges of the jar to hide the tape.

While a bunch of garden flowers arranged casually in a vase can be charming, most floral designers follow some basic rules in building an arrangement.

ABOVE: Though still useful, the widespread availability of florist's foam has turned flower frogs from everyday objects into collectibles. Glass and ceramic versions from such American makers as Heisey, Steuben, and McCoy are especially sought after; metal mesh frogs, mass produced in the early 1900s, are easier to find. All make decorative displays when not being used to anchor a bouquet.

Remember, however, that rules are made to be broken. Once you have a firm knowledge of the basic methods, you can improvise to express your own individuality and to make the best use of the materials at hand.

Make sure the vase you are planning to use has been thoroughly cleaned with soapy water and bleach to remove any bacteria. Put the (presoaked) foam, or whatever foundation you are using, in place and fill the vase with warm water to which you've already added plant food and a few drops of bleach. The bleach will help prevent the formation of bacteria that can clog stems. Stripping the stems of any leaves that will be beneath the water line as you work will also avoid bacterial buildup.

Before you place the first flower, have a clear picture of the finished bouquet in your mind. Will it be airy? Dense? Rounded? Geometric? Start by creating an "outline" of the size by setting a stem of one of the larger flowers in the center of the container to mark the height. As a rule of thumb, most arrangements range from one to two and a half times the height of the container. Now set one stem horizontally just above the rim of the container on all four sides to indicate the width. This measurement, somewhat freer, is determined visually. The

ABOVE: Betsy Yastrzemski assembles a bouquet of catmint, Mexican sage, artemesia, roses, and monkshood in her hand. Starting from the center, she works around the bouquet placing the herbs lower as she goes to form a dome. RIGHT: The final step is to cut the stems to one length so that the bouquet sits just at the top of the pitcher.

overall shape should be complementary to the container: the sturdier the container looks, the wider the bouquet can be without looking out of scale.

Next, begin filling in the arrangement, working with one type of flower or foliage at a time. Generally speaking, the larger flowers are put in place first, followed by smaller ones. Airy sprays like lady's mantle and spikes such as lavender and foxglove are added last. In the case of a small flower like lavender, you may want to group several flowers together to make a bigger impact and avoid "losing" them in the arrangement. Keep turning the arrangement as you work to avoid any holes and to be sure you are maintaining a good balance of small to large, of soft to sharp, and of color. Let some of the flowers and foliage trail over the edge for a more graceful look— and to hide any tape you may have used. The more symmetrical the arrangement, the more traditional

the result. If you want something more modern and dramatic, forsake symmetry.

The basic steps of the method just described work for most bouquets, with two exceptions. The first is a low arrangement, such as a centerpiece. Build this from the bottom up, covering the edge of the container first and then adding more flowers for height. Starting at the edge of the container and working up is also the way to go if you are planning a pyramid-shaped bouquet where larger flowers or even a bunch of grapes focuses attention at the bottom. The second exception is a dome arrangement, like those so popular in France. To fashion a dome, arrange the flowers in your hand with the stem end resting on the work surface. When you have achieved the look you want, tie the bunch together with raffia, then cut the stems to the desired length and pop them into the container. For a slightly different effect, and a prettier look if you are using a glass container where the stems become part of the arrangement, pivot the stems before placing them in the water. A simple bunch of country herbs and flowers can also be assembled this way.

No matter what kind of bouquet you're arranging, mist the flowers as you work to keep them fresh.

a nosegay
of sugars

Many people, especially bakers, keep a jar of vanilla-flavored sugar handy to impart extra flavor to baked goods and desserts. The herb garden is a source for more exotically flavored sugars. Imbued with the bouquet of such herbs as rose geranium, mint, lemon verbena, roses, or lavender, they will enhance the flavor of puddings, cakes, cookies, fruits, and teas.

1 cup fresh herb leaves or flowers

1 pound granulated sugar

Wash and thoroughly dry the herbs. Put the sugar in a bowl and stir in the herb leaves or flowers. Pour the sugar mixture into a jar with a tight-fitting lid and set aside for two weeks while the sugar absorbs the flavor. If desired, when using in a recipe, strain the leaves out of the amount of sugar needed.

BOUQUETS

THERE ARE CASUAL COUNTRY BOUQUETS,

strict minimalist displays, impressive formal arrangements, tiny nosegays, and special holiday decorations. All can be made more appealing through the use of herbal flowers and foliage.

casual bouquets

Whether it's a pitcherful of white feverfew or a row of blue enamelware filled with a variety of herbal flowers and foliage, a casual bouquet has a simple, just-picked-from-the-garden look. Often it is just that, but a simple, country bouquet can hide time and thought behind its nonchalant air.

A stroll through the garden in the early morning, or a visit to a local farmstand to see what is in bloom and what interesting and fragrant foliage is available, is just the beginning. Some thought must go into whether there are enough flowers for a showpiece bouquet or just a few blossoms for a tiny arrangement; whether it will be a play on one color or a kaleidoscope mix; whether it will be filled with flowers or mostly fragrant foliage. Perhaps one perfect poppy will find its way into an old bottle to set on the bathroom sink; a gathering of catmint, lavender, mint, and marjoram will produce a monochromatic bouquet for the guest room, or a clutch of sweet-smelling peonies will take a place of honor in the living room. The trick is to keep the flowers and the container simple.

PRECEDING PAGE: Ron Wendt, a New York City floral designer, uses the strength of three contrasting elements—bold artichokes, delicate lady's mantle, and lush monkshood—for a dramatic bouquet. RIGHT: Roberta Liford's garden is filled with roses of every type because "I haven't much time in July and August," she says, "and roses give the garden color all summer."

a hanging bouquet

What could be more appealing than coming upon a fragrant and colorful nosegay in an unexpected spot? With a hanging container, herbs and flowers can be suspended from a peg in the bathroom, on the door of a guest room, from a hook in the wall, or on a bookcase or cupboard. Although hanging vases are available commercially, creating your own is quick and easy.

materials

4 6-inch stalks of bamboo or dried fennel (or to size for your container)

Raffia

A lipped container, such as a jelly glass

White glue

❋ Measure the diameter of your container; cut each stalk so that it is 2 inches longer than the diameter.

❋ Overlap two stalks at right angles about 1 inch in from the end. Leaving a 3-inch tail, wind a length of raffia diagonally around the stalks in both directions to bind them together tightly. Tie a knot and trim the ends.

❋ Take a third stalk and, using the glass below the lip as a size guide, attach this stalk to the end of one of the first stalks in the same manner. Be sure to attach it above or below the other stalk to match the opposite side. Repeat with the fourth stalk, being sure to measure carefully so that the rim of the glass will rest securely on the frame. To further stabilize the frame, add a bit of white glue to the raffia at each corner to prevent it from slipping.

❋ To make the hanging support, take 10 strips of raffia a little more than twice the length you want the hanger to be and twist them together to form a thick "rope." Knot one end around one corner of the frame and the other on the opposite corner. Slip the glass into the frame and fill with water and flowers.

urbane bouquets

Whether it's to be placed in a formal room, be set on a buffet at an important dinner, or act as a focal point on the mantel, there are times when a bouquet is called upon to add drama and elegance to a room. Size is often the key to making these bouquets more than casual; so is the choice of a container. While silver, fine porcelain, and other rich materials almost ensure that a bouquet will be able to take its place in the most formal setting, the surprise of a polished bouquet in a basket or other informal container can be very refreshing.

More often than not, an urbane bouquet is composed of a dense array of flowers symmetrically arranged, but a few dramatic stems of angelica or bamboo set in a simple architectural vase can be just as striking. In these more sophisticated presentations the use of color is more studied; the richness of material is sometimes overwhelming, and occasionally exotic. Imagine a plethora of roses set in an antique porcelain footbath, a few dramatic stalks of foxglove arching out of a trumpet-shaped glass vase, or a mix of colorful herbal flowers and greenery in a silver urn. To be assured of success, start with a beautiful container and an assortment of more sophisticated flowers and greenery, then fashion them into an abundant bouquet along traditional lines or a modern minimalist display where the shapes of the stems, flowers, and foliage are displayed in all their architectural beauty.

Minimalist bouquets, using just one herb or flower in simple, often architectural arrangements, work especially well in modern settings and emphasize the sculptural beauty of the flower. A refreshing change to mixed arrangements, they can give even the most common flower a new look like the fountain of foxgloves, LEFT, or bring less often used herbs like angelica, RIGHT, into the living room. Using multiples of geometric vases or bottles containing the same flowers or foliage, or a different flower in each, is another approach.

Blantyre is a renowned country hotel that sits among eighty-five acres in the Berkshires. Close to the Tudor-style mansion, a series of gardens yield flowers for the lovely bouquets that fill the rooms. The lady's mantle, lamb's ears, peonies, and astilbe from the garden are supplemented by such unusual plants as wild mustard, elder-flower, cardoons, and wild roses. Each bouquet is designed with a particular room in mind—while the imposing dining and sitting rooms require large, formal arrangements, the bedrooms are graced with softer, more romantic bouquets like these.

When floral designer Ron Wendt begins to work, he considers the season as well as the person for whom the arrangement is being done. BELOW LEFT: During the fall, he might choose a copper pot as a container because of its warm color, then fill it with plants with hardy textures such as hypernicum, lamb's ears, and porcelain berries and contrasting colors such as the acid yellow of lady's mantle, pink roses, and maroon dahlias. BELOW RIGHT: For a gentleman's bathroom, he likes the simple, strong masculinity of gray artemesia massed in a cashepot. "I like the great structure in herbal foliage," he says. LEFT: Even "weeds" such as pokeberry are turned into simple nosegays during the season.

special-occasion bouquets

Throughout the years, bouquets of herbs and flowers have been an indispensable part of rites and celebrations as well as a means to convey a message of friendship and love. Surely no holiday would be complete without a seasonal bouquet, and no matter what the holiday, herbs, either fresh or dried, help proclaim the spirit of the season. In the fall, goldenrod, bittersweet, sage, and yarrow are among those herbs whose warm colors reflect the season. On Valentine's Day, a bountiful bouquet of red roses signifying love or a fragrant bunch of violets sending a message of loyalty and steadfastness will warm the heart of the recipient. For the Fourth of July, set the picnic table with a red, white, and blue centerpiece of poppies, feverfew, and cornflowers. And at Christmas mix herbs such as thyme, bay, and rosemary with traditional holiday greens like juniper, pine, boxwood, holly, and mistletoe, which are herbal, too. Adding silvery artemesia and rosy rose hips, and even some dried hydrangea sprayed with gold paint, along with fruits, nuts, and cones, will produce glorious holiday decorations.

Weddings offer a splendid opportunity to take advantage of the beauty and symbolism of herbal bouquets. Ivy (marriage), jasmine (happiness and joy), lavender (luck), myrtle (love and fertility), rosemary (remembrance), and sage (domestic tranquillity) are a few of the herbs that add both beauty and sentiment to bridal bouquets. These same herbs can also be mixed into a fragrant and colorful potpourri to throw at the bride and groom in lieu of rice.

RIGHT: When the herb garden is in full bloom, gather culinary herbs such as basil, marjoram, catmint, and mint along with edible flowering herbs like roses and lavender to make a fragrant cook's bouquet to adorn the table or give to a friend. To display the bouquet in a basket, arrange the herbs in a plastic or glass container that fits into the basket.

Herbal bouquets are also a joyful offering for any occasion that calls for a kind thought. Take inspiration from the Victorians, who conveyed their feelings through the language of flowers, weaving herbal leaves and flowers into a nosegay that professed love (basil), happiness (marjoram), or enchantment (lemon verbena) or even negative sentiments such as affectation (nasturtium), fickleness (foxglove), or distrust (lavender).

Take advantage of the many wonderful qualities of herbs to personalize bouquets. Add rosemary and thyme, both disinfectants, to a bouquet for a sick friend to help freshen the air, or make a fresh or dried culinary bouquet for a cook.

Jennifer Hauser, a floral/event designer on Long Island, often receives requests for an herbal wedding. "Herbs look wonderful all mixed together," she says. "I love the juxtaposition of roses with the green of mint. It's all very natural and lends itself to a country wedding." PRECEDING PAGE: Weaving such herbs as lamb's ears, oregano, lavender, roses, hydrangea, and peonies together, she fashions lush centerpieces and, LEFT, bouquets for the bride and bridesmaids. ABOVE RIGHT: Lavender and oregano are even spun into boutonnieres for the ushers. RIGHT: Silver julep cups stuffed with lavender are placed wherever needed for extra fragrance and beauty.

Making an herbal Christmas tree can be as simple as tucking dried herbal flowers and foliage between the branches of an evergreen and draping rich gold ribbon from the top. Wreaths can be hung on a tree or inside a window, or they can even be placed on the table as a centerpiece. For a change, mass green apples with juniper, rosehips, and dried garlic chive blossoms in an Oriental container or pile herb-covered styrofoam balls, holly, ornaments, and pine cones on a silver tray.

aromatic herbal paper

Small bits of dried herbs and flowers can be salvaged and transformed into splendid hand-made paper for writing notes, wrapping presents, or even covering books or boxes.

materials

Wood-framed drying screen (a small window screen will do)

A sink or tub large enough to hold the screen flat

Blender

Paper (white or colored tissue paper works well)

Fresh or dried herbs and flowers

Dish towels

Sponge

Blotter paper (several pieces)

Rolling pin

Gelatin (optional)

* Place the screen in a sink or bathtub. Hold it down and pour in enough water to come halfway up the side of the screen. Fill the blender two-thirds full with lukewarm water. Add an equal amount of paper; let it soak up the water for a minute. Blend on low for 10 seconds, then on high for 30 seconds. Add herbs and flowers during the blending. The later you add them, the larger the pieces will be.

* Hold the screen horizontally; distribute the pulp evenly over the screen. A large screen might need several batches of pulp. Lift the screen straight up and allow it to drip for a few minutes.

* Set the screen on the spread-out dish towels and press out excess water with the dampened sponge. Lay a sheet of blotter paper over the herbal paper and flip the screen over so the herbal paper rests on the blotter paper. Sponge out more water.

* Turn the herbal paper over onto a new dry piece of blotter paper; press more water out of the blotting paper sandwich with a rolling pin. Replace the top blotter with a dry one, flip, and roll again. Repeat several times.

* Remove the top piece of blotting paper and gently lift the damp sheet of paper. Set it to dry on any flat waterproof surface.

* To use the paper for writing, dip the dry sheets in a solution of 1 tablespoon gelatin dissolved in 1/2 cup hot water and diluted with 3 cups cold water.

caring for your bouquets

A little common sense will ensure that your herbal bouquets continue to give you maximum pleasure the longest possible time. Keep the bouquets in a cool place and mist them with warm water occasionally to keep them fresh. Avoid placing them on or near a radiator or in the bright sunlight, especially in summer, unless you are trying to force flowers open. Air-conditioning and drafts are also detrimental to their long life. If you have the time and energy, moving bouquets to a cool basement or outdoors (when it's not freezing) for the night will prolong their life, since cool temperatures and darkness slow down the opening of the flowers.

Refill the container that holds your bouquet with cold water every day. Certain flowers will drink more than others, and the weather will also affect the rate at which the water evaporates. Every several days replace the water completely, add more plant food, remove all dead leaves and flowers, and recut the stems. Since some flowers naturally last longer than others, you can prolong the life of a bouquet by choosing flowers with different life spans and replacing the wilted flowers with fresh blooms. If you start with reasonably tall flowers, you can keep trimming the stems until the bouquet begins to look tired, and then dismantle the bouquet and remake the usable flowers into a smaller arrangement. Repeat this procedure until you have just a few pretty flowers left: Place them in a bud vase or create a mini-arrangement for a desk or dressing table and continue to enjoy them.

If roses begin to wilt, try placing the blossoms

LEFT: A painter as well as a gardener, Linda Williams visualizes her bouquet before starting. "Not each individual flower," she says, "but the overall shape. And I faintly bear in mind where the bouquet will go." She wanders through her extensive gardens at Marle Place in Kent, England, picking whatever herbs and flowers take her fancy, then assembles them into glorious bouquets like this one in an old butter churn.

in a bath of cool water, their stems covered with a towel. This allows them to absorb water through all the pores and often revives them nicely.

a growing bouquet

Gardening in pots has roots in antiquity. The atria and balconies of ancient Rome were decorated with terra-cotta pots, and aromatic herb- and flower-filled pots lined the paths of Persia's fabled water gardens. Fifteenth-century Italians filled tubs with such fragrant herbs as violets and basil and even grew citrus trees in pots. These "potted gardens" had the added advantage of enabling the gardener to bring the plants indoors during the cold winter months, a system the English adopted with enthusiasm in the seventeenth century.

Container gardening is a necessity for those with little space or limited sun or for those who want to grow shade-loving plants but have little shade. Lush flowering pots are also an excellent way to soften stone patios, to highlight a specific spot in the garden, or to contain aggressive plants such as bamboo. Moreover, containers enable you to experiment with new plants and plant combinations without disturbing the garden. They are also a good way to grow seasonal plants or those for which you have no room in the garden. A collection of scented geraniums and a bay tree underplanted with Corsican mint are good examples.

The choice of containers for a growing bouquet is extensive: Anything that will hold soil will do as long as it has drainage holes. Among the traditional choices are oversized terra-cotta pots, both plain and fancy; wooden boxes and barrels; concrete planters; lead or other metal boxes and urns; lightweight fiberglass pots; and window boxes of every type. They can be used singly or massed together for greater impact.

HERBS

LEFT: Make a miniature garden in a barrel such as this fragrance garden with pineapple mint, thyme, lavender, heliotrope, lemon verbena, and sage. Nasturtiums and calendula add color. BELOW: Landscape designer Lisa Stamm uses imaginatively planted pots as decorative accents. The varied colors and textures of such plants as sweet potato vine, nicotiana, artemesia, and nasturtiums are eye-catching even when flowers are at a minimum.

LEFT: Troughs of granite, lava stone, or hypertufa (a mixture of cement, sand, and peat moss) are another option for container planting. Originally designed for rocky alpine plants, they are equally suitable for herbs that prefer dry soil. BELOW: A window box should be treated in the same way as any other container. Place plants as much as one third closer together for a lush effect as in this example designed by Colleen Chaisty.

Attend flea markets and yard sales with an open mind: Old tins, crates, and washtubs are among the items you can convert to a planter. Or go to your local stoneworks and buy a series of terra-cotta chimney pots in different sizes and group them together.

Decide if you want your planter to be movable or a permanent part of your garden. One of the advantages of growing container bouquets, of course, is the opportunity to have plants on view only when they are at the peak of their bloom. Those in movable containers can then be cut back and the pot moved to a less obvious spot, or you can transplant the spent plant into the garden and replace it with a fresh one. Permanent pots are best planted with a grouping of herbs and flowers that will perform all season. Keep them in good shape by pruning, feeding, and watering them regularly.

With water running through the soil on a regular basis, container plantings require more feeding than those in the garden. Fertilize with diluted fish emulsion when you plant, then continue to feed them every two weeks during the growing season. Because pots, especially the terra-cotta variety, dry out more quickly than in-ground plantings, they need to be watered more. The smaller the pot, the faster it will dry out. Always water until the water runs out the bottom of the container.

Good drainage and strong root development are especially important for potted plants, so use a soilless planting medium or a light potting soil. You also might want to include some polymer granules in the soil mix to help it retain moisture. Before planting, put a piece of broken crockery, some pebbles, or a piece of screening over the drainage holes to keep soil from leaking out. Fill the container to within one inch of the top with premoistened soil mix. If you're using a very large pot or a barrel, fill the bottom half with plastic peanuts before putting in the soil.

This conserves soil and also keeps the pot from being too heavy. If you are using a crate, a basket, or any less-than-watertight container, line it with moss first and then a heavy-gauge plastic bag. Be sure to punch drainage holes in the bag and then trim it to just below the rim of the container.

Now you are ready to add herbs. As with a regular bouquet, consider the size and shape of the container in choosing the plants. A good rule of thumb is to have the overall planting anywhere from two to five times the height of the pot, although a washtub overflowing with low-growing pansies has a charm of its own. A lush planting of a single herbal flower is as appealing as a more ambitious planting with a tall plant, such as fennel in the center surrounded by mid-sized herbs like sage and edged with cascading plants such as thyme and nasturtiums.

In planning your growing bouquets, consider the juxtaposition of texture, foliage, and color. Think about using white-flowered or silver-leaved plants to brighten a dark corner; contrast bright green or yellow foliage with deeper greens; use all one family of color in the flowers or an exciting contrast; play sharp needle-leafed herbs like rosemary against those with large soft leaves like lamb's ears. Or consider planting a tub with all different varieties of one herb, such as lavender, sage, or oregano.

When winter comes, discard any annuals. Take perennial pots indoors or set them in a heated garage or shed. If you want to leave them outdoors, insulate the pots carefully with leaves and burlap or with one of the commercial wraps available, or dig them into the ground to protect the roots from freezing.

Take care of your potted garden and it will reward you with an ever-changing display. Harvest your herbs liberally and deadhead flowers regularly. They will be fuller and flower more, offering you greater enjoyment of your live bouquet.

may wine

Sweet woodruff's spiraling whorls of deep green leaves topped with bright white flowers are symbolic of springtime. While this fragrant herb makes a pretty little bouquet, it is better known for the part it plays in the celebration of May Day. In the Rhine Valley, woodruff is traditionally gathered in woods and forests to flavor the Mai Wein Bowle. As it wilts and dries, the fragrance of coumarin, a pleasant mix of new-mown hay and vanilla, develops. It is this distinctive flavor that enhances the May wine, a flavor, incidentally, that connoisseurs look for in certain fine white wines. While a Rhine Riesling is the traditional base for May wine, any light white wine can be substituted. In America, brandy and/or champagne are often added to make a May Punch Bowl. Serve May wine at any informal gathering, pouring it from a pitcher or ladling it from a punch bowl. Toss in a few johnny-jump-ups or strawberries as decoration.

1 small bunch of sweet woodruff (2 to 3 sprays)

3 tablespoons fine granulated sugar

1 bottle of white wine, preferably Riesling or a light spring wine

Ice cubes

Johnny-jump-ups or strawberries (optional)

Place the woodruff in a nonreactive container with a tight-fitting cover. Sprinkle with the sugar. Add 1 cup of the wine, cover, and let steep for several hours or overnight.

When ready to serve, filter the wine into a punch bowl or pitcher. Add the remaining wine. Add ice and sprinkle with johnny-jump-ups, if desired. Let stand for 15 minutes before serving. Place a strawberry in each glass, if desired.

INDEX